THE COLORFUL WORLD OF
DINOSAURS

MATT SEWELL

Princeton Architectural Press

New York

For Romy and Mae, Eve and Fin, and Arlo

CONTENTS

INTRODUCTION

Welcome to the amazing world of the dinosaurs!

We all know dinosaurs. They were the rulers of the planet. They are the monsters from the movies. They are the bones we see in the museums.

But do we really know them? Can we imagine what they looked like? What they sounded like? What they smelled like?

In the following pages, find out why *Stegosaurus* had spikes, fear *Spinosaurus* stomping through the swamp, and get to know some of the closest cousins of our modern-day birds—*Archaeopteryx* and *Troodon.*

A Note on the Illustrations

We have always been told that dinosaurs looked like big lizards with muddy brown or boring green scales. No longer! Some smart paleontologists (to you or me, scientists that study fossils) now think that many dinosaurs may have been colorful. Not only that, but a lot of them may have had feathers. The illustrations on the following pages have been inspired by these ideas—helping you to really imagine the bright, scary world of the distant past.

Dinosaur Groups and Families

Paleontologists have identified more than one thousand dinosaur species, and there probably were thousands more. With so many dinos to track, it's no wonder that scientists have divided them up into groups.

Grouping species is called *taxonomy*. The taxonomy of dinosaurs has changed over the years as more and more fossils are discovered, but scientists can agree on the main dinosaur groups:

Ceratopsians—horned and ruffed
Sauropods—long-necked plant-eaters
Stegosaurs—spiked and plated
Ankylosaurs—armored plant-eaters
Hadrosaurs—duck-billed
Theropods—two-legged meat-eaters (mostly!)

These groups can be split further into families. The theropods make up a good example group due to their range in size, diet, and appearance.

Theropod families include:

Oviraptorids—toothless and parrotlike
Ornithomimosaurs—fast and ostrichlike
Velociraptors—vicious, they hunt in packs
Tyrannosaurs—large, terrifying predators

Confusingly, the well-known flying pterosaurs and swimming ichthyosaurs do not have dinosaur families. In fact, they are not dinosaurs at all. We have included them in this book because they would have been a common sight during the time of the dinosaurs and shared their ecosystems.

DID YOU KNOW?

Modern-day birds are descendants of theropods. Fortunately, they're much less scary than their ancestors.

Dinosaur Diets

The different types of dinosaurs ate a lot of different types of food. The massive *Argentinosaurus* would not have eaten the same food as the small *Velociraptor,* and the slow-footed *Tyrannosaurus rex* would not have munched the same fare as the nimble *Troodon.* These changes in diet would have been due to a number of reasons, from the physical—such as size and shape—to the environmental—such as climate and location.

Dino diets can be described using the terms below.

Carnivorous—meat eating
Herbivorous—plant eating
Omnivorous—meat and plant eating
Piscivorous—fish eating
Insectivorous—insect eating

DID YOU KNOW?

Brachiosaurus (see page 54) would have had to eat four hundred pounds of plants a day to maintain its weight— that's a whole lot of leaves!

Dinosaur Times and Climates

Dinosaurs roamed the earth for more than 160 million years. It's no wonder they were able to develop into different shapes and sizes and had different diets over all that time. The key dinosaur time periods are the Triassic, Jurassic, and Cretaceous eras:

Period	Time	Climate and environment
Triassic	252–201 million years ago	Warm, dry deserts
Jurassic	201–145 million years ago	Warmer, wet rain forests
Cretaceous	145–66 million years ago	Warm, wet, and floral

Over millions of years, the different climates changed dinosaur life in a multitude of ways. The Triassic deserts produced little vegetation for the early dinosaurs, so herbivores, and therefore carnivores, were small and light. The Jurassic was the age of warm, lush rain forests—and more food meant that little dinosaurs could evolve into big ones. Then, during the Cretaceous period, flowers and increased volcanic activity influenced dinosaur life even further.

Then 66 million years ago, BANG! The dinosaurs were extinct. Most scientists think this was caused by an enormous asteroid from outer space blasting into Earth. Others reckon volcanic eruptions or climate change was to blame.

Now the time has come to bring these monsters back to life.
Are you brave enough to turn the page?

DID YOU KNOW?

Large, terrifying beasts weren't limited to the Triassic, Jurassic, and Cretaceous periods. *Basilosaurus* (see page 76) was a monstrous early whale that stalked the waters of the Eocene period twenty-five million years after the death of the dinosaurs.

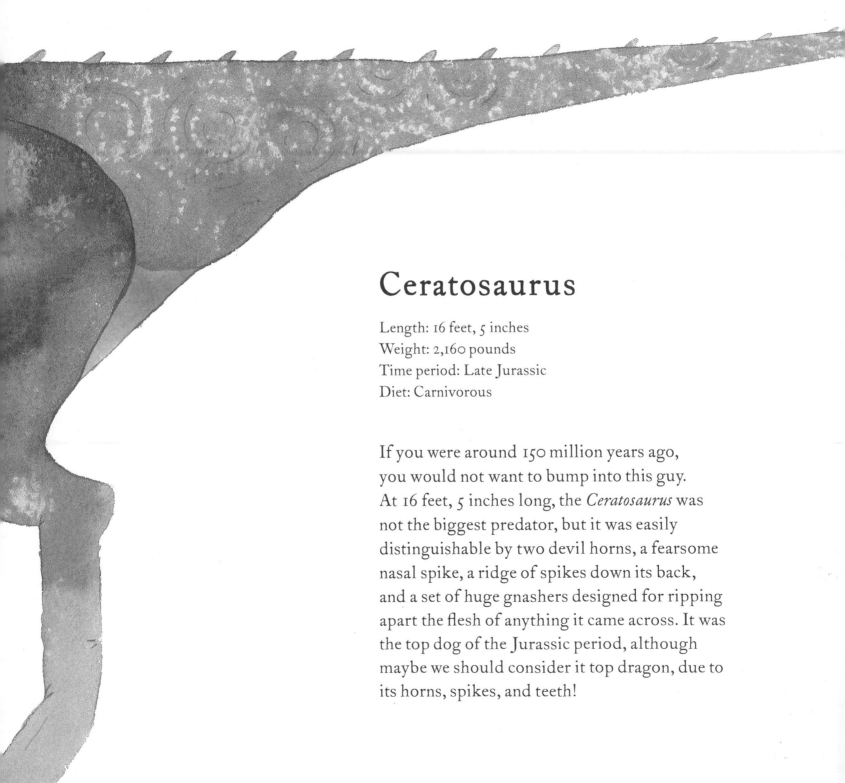

Ceratosaurus

Length: 16 feet, 5 inches
Weight: 2,160 pounds
Time period: Late Jurassic
Diet: Carnivorous

If you were around 150 million years ago,
you would not want to bump into this guy.
At 16 feet, 5 inches long, the *Ceratosaurus* was
not the biggest predator, but it was easily
distinguishable by two devil horns, a fearsome
nasal spike, a ridge of spikes down its back,
and a set of huge gnashers designed for ripping
apart the flesh of anything it came across. It was
the top dog of the Jurassic period, although
maybe we should consider it top dragon, due to
its horns, spikes, and teeth!

Stegosaurus

Length: 30 feet
Weight: 15,450 pounds
Time period: Late Jurassic
Diet: Herbivorous

This famous dinosaur's row of armored plates makes it easily recognizable. There's no need to be scared of this peaceful herbivore; however, you wouldn't want a thirty-foot-long vegetarian standing on your foot.

As well as its shield plates, *Stegosaurus* was well defended with tail spikes. These fierce weapons made them difficult prey for the predators of the Jurassic period, such as the fearsome *Ceratosaurus*.

Pterodactylus
and Batrachognathus

Wingspan: 3 feet, 3 inches to 5 feet
Weight: 2 pounds, 3 ounces to 11 pounds
Time period: Late Jurassic
Diet: Carnivorous and piscivorous

Wingspan: 1 foot, 7 1/2 inches
Weight: 5 1/4 ounces
Time period: Late Jurassic
Diet: Insectivorous

Pterodactyl is the common family name for pterosaurs, the flying animals that dominated the skies of the Jurassic period. This *Pterodactylus*, one of many pterodactyls, was not even half the size of the giant pterosaurs that lived millions of years later in the Cretaceous period. Still, *Pterodactylus* enjoyed streamlined flight with wings the same shape as a bird's, only made of skin stretched from the armpits, wrists, and fingers. Ingenious!

Batrachognathus was a pterosaur family member that was basically a head on wings. Not much bigger than a blackbird, these little pocket rockets were perfectly designed for catching big juicy insects above the steamy Jurassic swamps. Munch, munch, crunch.

Sphaerotholus

Length: Estimated 6 feet
Weight: Estimated 550 pounds
Time period: Late Cretaceous
Diet: Herbivorous

By the Late Cretaceous period, dinosaurs
had developed all kinds of fancy appendages
and armor, like this bonehead *Sphaerotholus*
with its turtle-shell bicycle helmet. It's no
wonder that its name literally translates
as "ball dome," because *Sphaerotholus* are
thought to have swung their helmeted
heads in defense, using them as pummeling
wrecking balls against savage attackers. It
is also assumed that they would clash their
domes together, fighting for supremacy
among their peers.

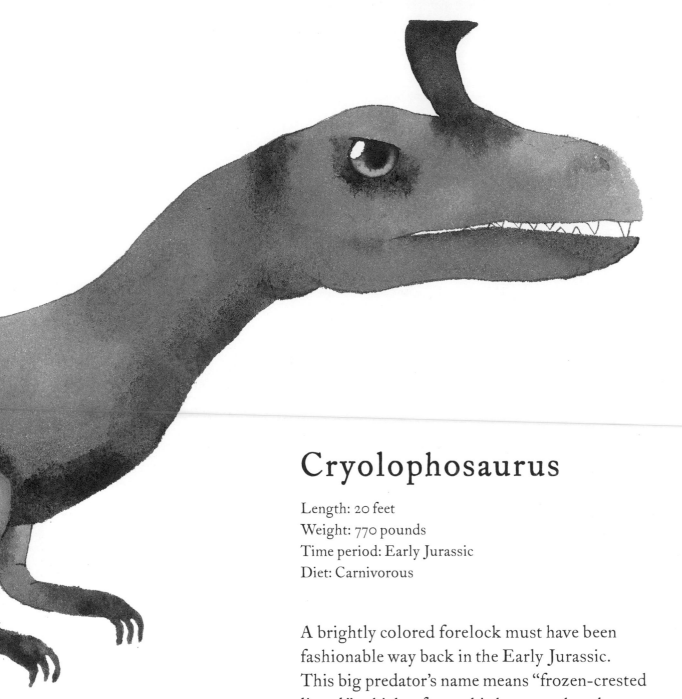

Cryolophosaurus

Length: 20 feet
Weight: 770 pounds
Time period: Early Jurassic
Diet: Carnivorous

A brightly colored forelock must have been fashionable way back in the Early Jurassic. This big predator's name means "frozen-crested lizard," which refers to his home, rather than his hairstyle! Fossilized remains have been found near the South Pole, but this doesn't mean *Cryolophosaurus* was a cold-climate hunter. Dinosaurs lived so long ago that the continents were in different shapes, and so the land mass that is Antarctica was much farther north, in the sunny supercontinent Gondwana. It's amazing the difference a couple hundred million years can make.

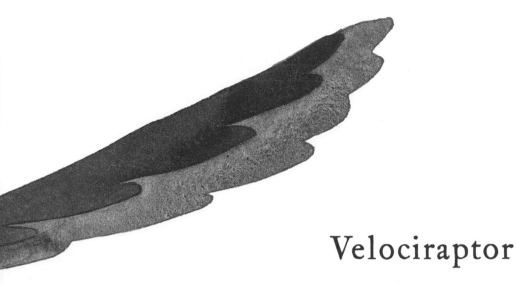

Velociraptor

Length: 6 feet, 8 inches
Weight: 35 pounds
Time period: Late Cretaceous
Diet: Carnivorous

Many people disagree about how some dinosaurs looked and acted, and one of the most divisive is the famous *Velociraptor*. It would be easy to imagine them as raging lizards, capable of bringing down the enormous sauropods, but their appearance could have been more similar to that of odd-looking birds. Very odd birds—*Velociraptor* was the size of a turkey, but no turkey has sharp teeth and a disemboweling claw on each feathered foot. These razor-sharp weapons, and the long tail for balancing, made *Velociraptor* and its pack formidable predators. Ambushed by a gang of fancy turkeys—what a way to go!

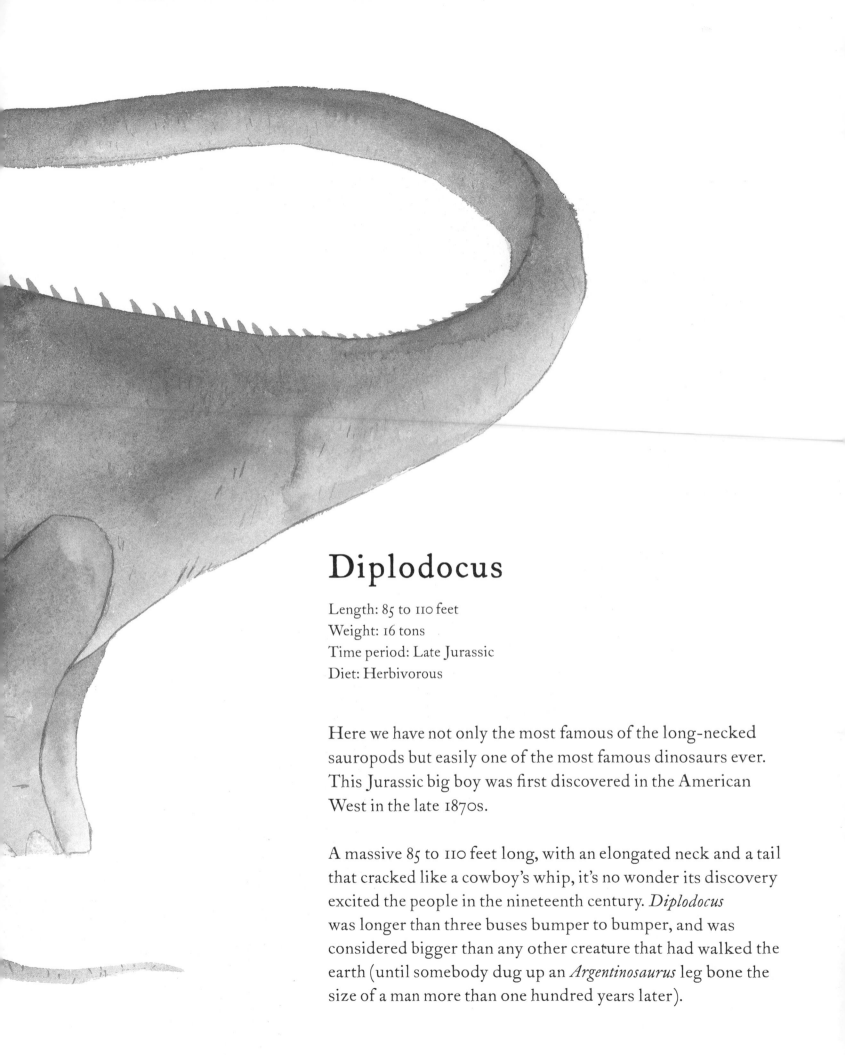

Diplodocus

Length: 85 to 110 feet
Weight: 16 tons
Time period: Late Jurassic
Diet: Herbivorous

Here we have not only the most famous of the long-necked sauropods but easily one of the most famous dinosaurs ever. This Jurassic big boy was first discovered in the American West in the late 1870s.

A massive 85 to 110 feet long, with an elongated neck and a tail that cracked like a cowboy's whip, it's no wonder its discovery excited the people in the nineteenth century. *Diplodocus* was longer than three buses bumper to bumper, and was considered bigger than any other creature that had walked the earth (until somebody dug up an *Argentinosaurus* leg bone the size of a man more than one hundred years later).

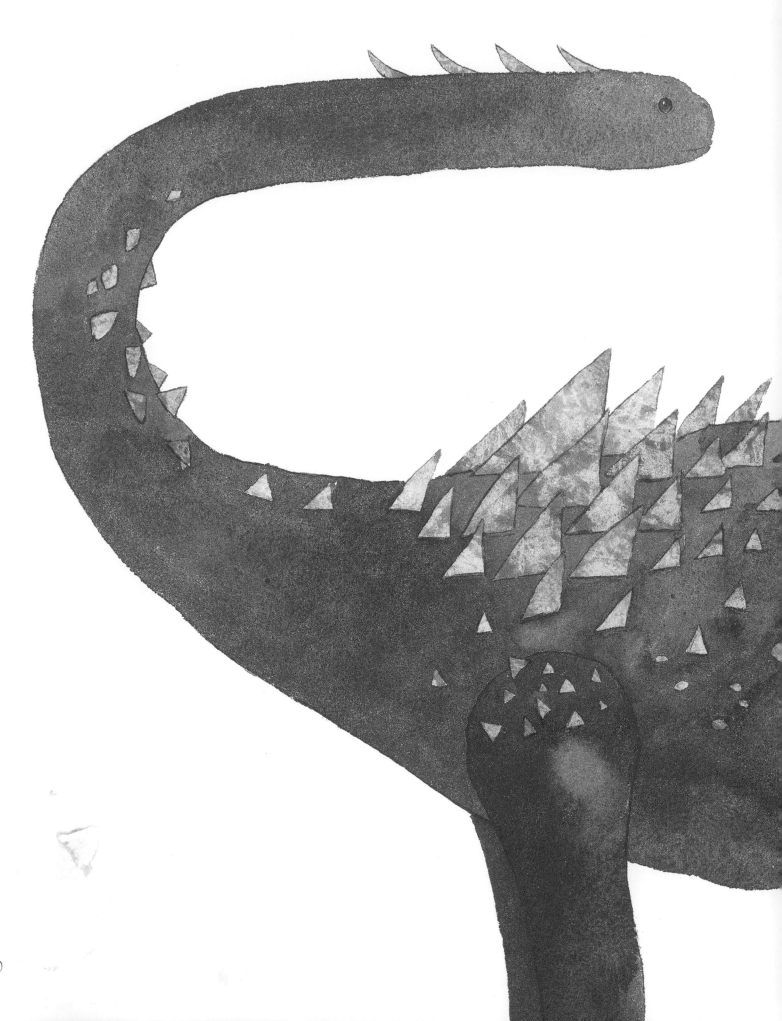

Ampelosaurus

Length: 50 feet
Weight: 5,500 pounds
Time period: Late Cretaceous
Diet: Herbivorous

Titanosaurs were large sauropods that flourished worldwide during the Late Cretaceous period; of these, *Ampelosaurus* was one of the smallest.

These dinosaurs were notable for being found in continental Europe, particularly France, the place that gives them the nickname "vineyard lizard." Like *Argentinosaurus*, its massve cousin, *Ampelosaurus* was suited in armor of plates and spikes—protection necessary for the period's deadly dangers.

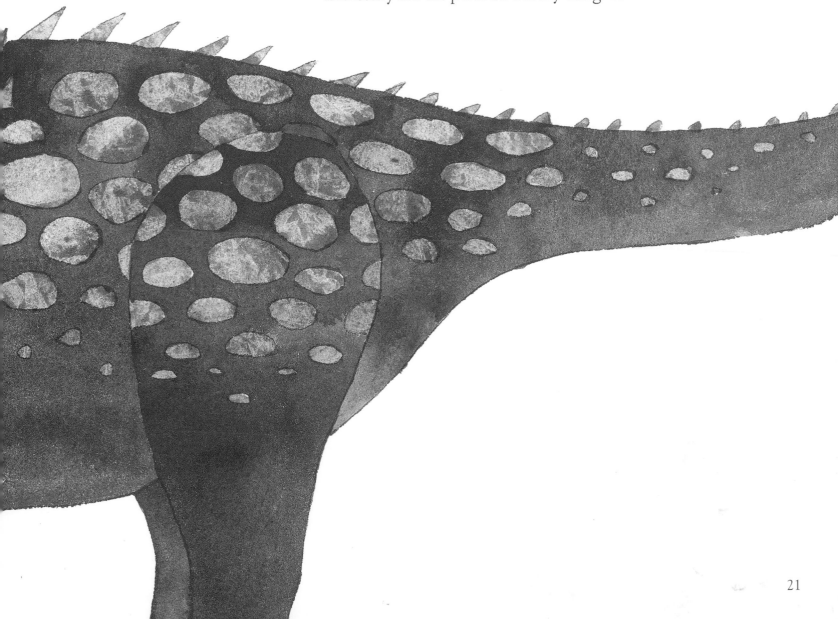

Sharovipteryx

Length: 8 inches
Weight: ¼ ounce
Time period: Middle Triassic
Diet: Omnivorous

Old stretchy here, a reptilian cousin of
the dinosaurs, had a unique take on flight
compared with the later forearm-winged
pterosaurs. *Sharovipteryx* used its hind legs
as wings, and this unique trait probably
ended with this creature—only one set of
fossils has ever been found. Splat!

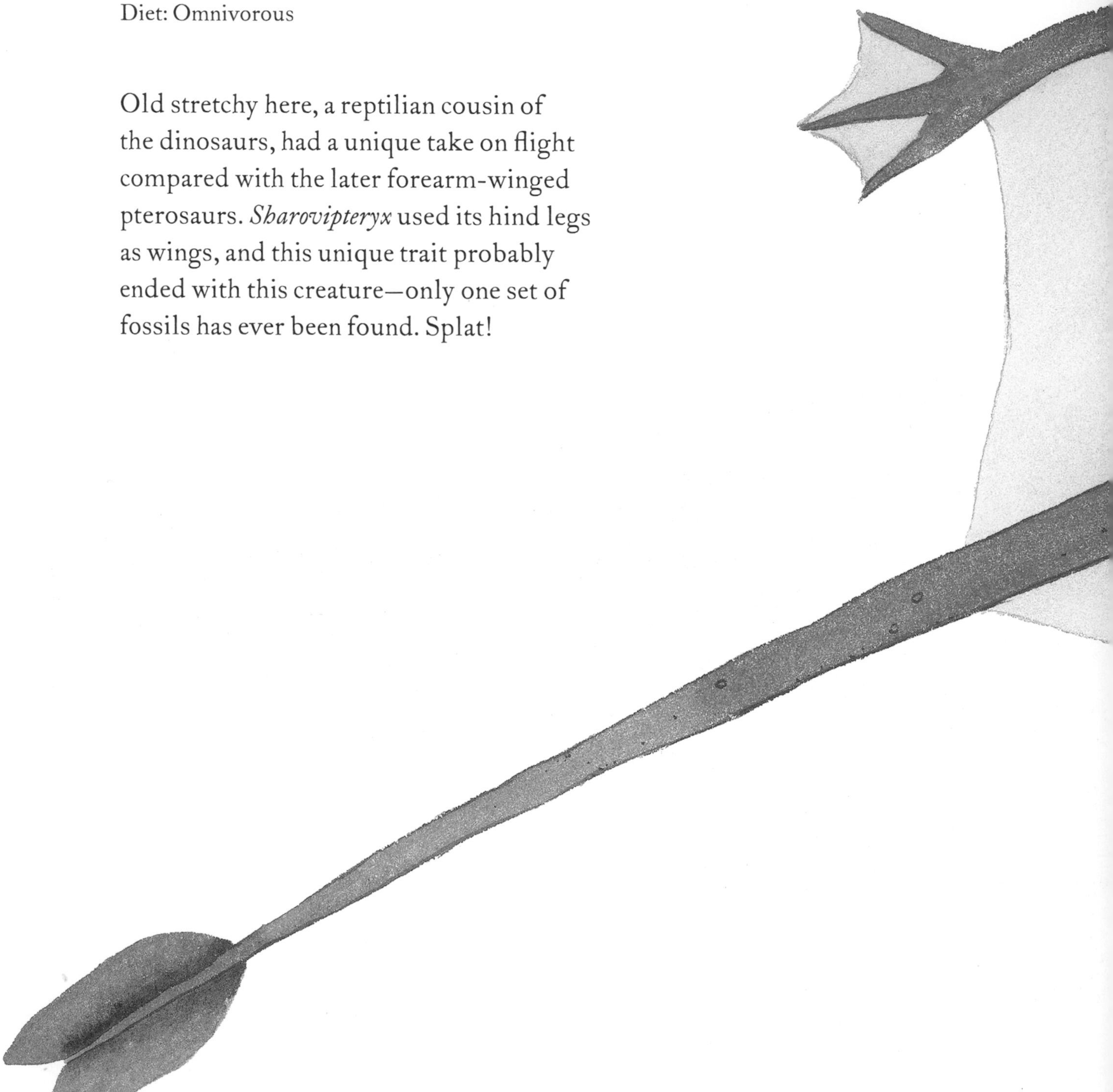

Ichthyosaurs

Length: 3 feet, 3 inches to 55 feet
Weight: 2 pounds, 2 ounces to 1 ton
Time period: Early Triassic–Middle Cretaceous
Diet: Carnivorous and piscivorous

Five hundred million years ago, fish evolved
to grow limbs, breathe air, and leave the ocean.
One or two of these fish-turned-reptiles must
have been bored on dry land, because some
returned to the open ocean and developed into
Ichthyosaurs and other underwater reptiles.
These talented swimmers of the Triassic,
Jurassic, and Cretaceous periods are unrelated
to sharks and dolphins, despite sharing a similar
traditional shape.

Utahraptor

Length: 20 feet
Weight: 2,200 pounds
Time period: Early Cretaceous
Diet: Carnivorous

Related to *Velociraptor*, *Utahraptor* was given its name because its remains were discovered in Utah. It was bigger, badder, and uglier than the rest of the *Velociraptor* family. *Utahraptor* stood at an imposing 6 feet, 8 inches high and was more than twenty feet long, making it more than three times the size of its deadly cousin. It was also covered in feathers and had fearsome teeth and claws—*Utahraptor's* sickle claw was nearly as big as this book! Stocky and massive, this brute was built for strength, and it was fast and cunning too.

So, if you find yourself in a difficult situation with a *Utahraptor*, you should run (or perhaps bury your head in the sand and hope he goes away)!

Iguanodon

Length: 35 feet
Weight: 9 tons
Time period: Early Cretaceous
Diet: Herbivorous

The huge thirty-five-foot *Iguanodon* was the first scientifically recognized dinosaur. It was discovered in the early nineteenth century in southern England. By the 1880s, it had captured the public's imagination— so much that it was one of the most famous dinosaurs in the world.

During those early years after its discovery, *Iguanodon's* thumb spike was a mystery and was originally placed on his nose, rhino style. It is now believed to have been used as a handy tool or a much-needed dagger.

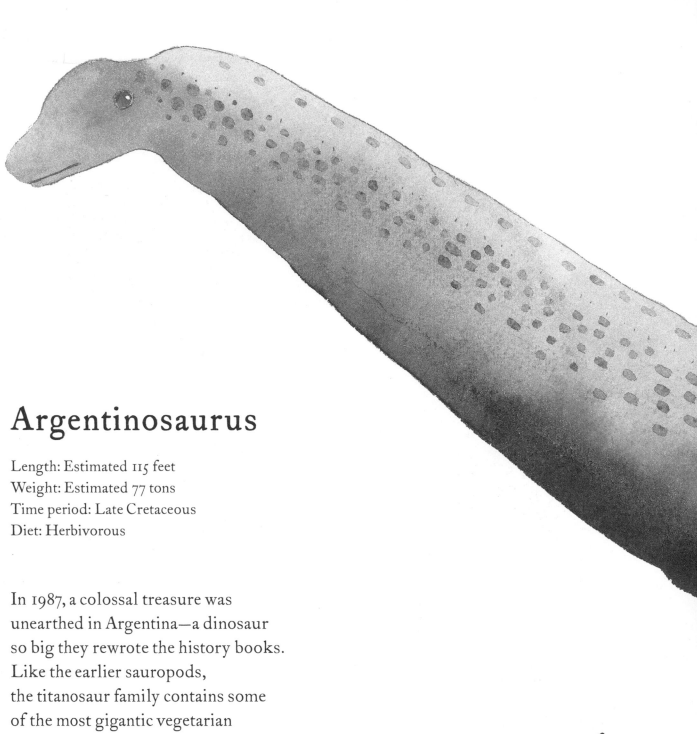

Argentinosaurus

Length: Estimated 115 feet
Weight: Estimated 77 tons
Time period: Late Cretaceous
Diet: Herbivorous

In 1987, a colossal treasure was
unearthed in Argentina—a dinosaur
so big they rewrote the history books.
Like the earlier sauropods,
the titanosaur family contains some
of the most gigantic vegetarian
dinosaurs ever discovered, and
Argentinosaurus is the biggest and
heaviest yet. Breaking all records by
measuring in at about 115 feet long,
this dinosaur was as heavy as a herd of
elephants! *Argentinosaurus* must have
flattened forests as it pounded
the ground as a peaceful yet
unstoppable force.

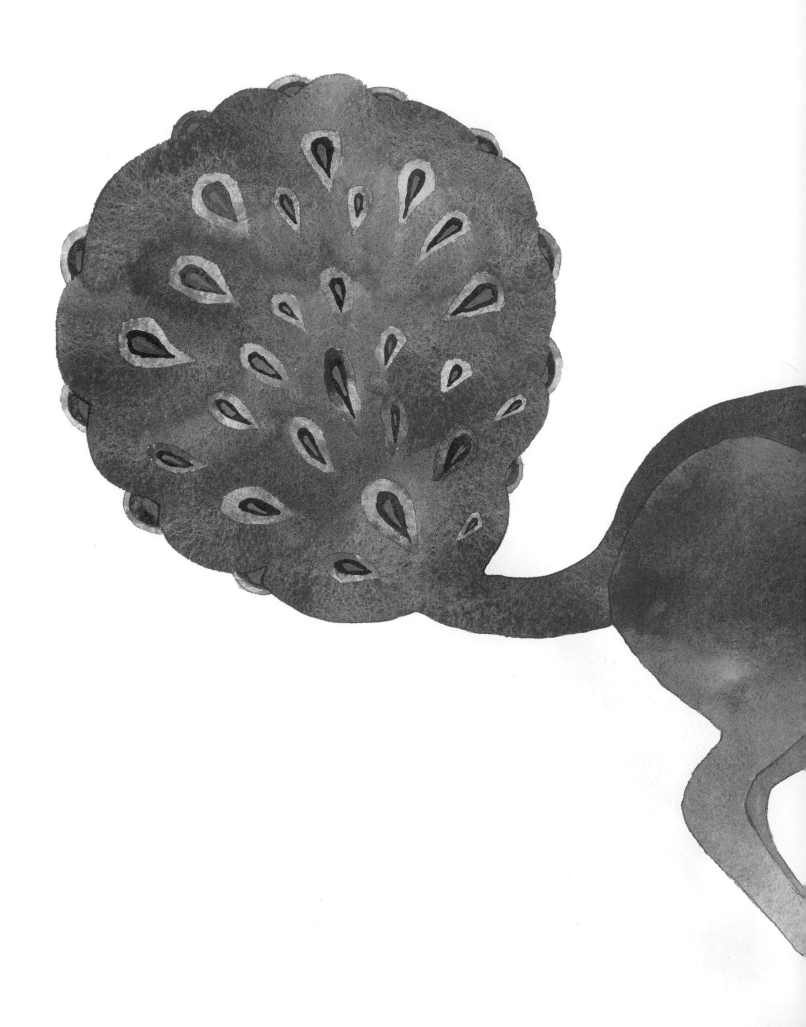

Nomingia

Length: 5 feet, 3 inches
Weight: 80 pounds
Time period: Late Cretaceous
Diet: Omnivorous

Rocks from the Cretaceous period show many dinosaurs with birdlike features, such as the oviraptorids. The oviraptorid family would have been similar to the big flightless birds we know now—today's Australian cassowary even has a bright head crest and a *Velociraptor* claw! *Nomingia* had another spectacular bird trait—an elaborate fan of feathers. He must have displayed this for courtship, like a peacock, or for intimidation, like an owl, but on a much larger scale. What a sight that must have been!

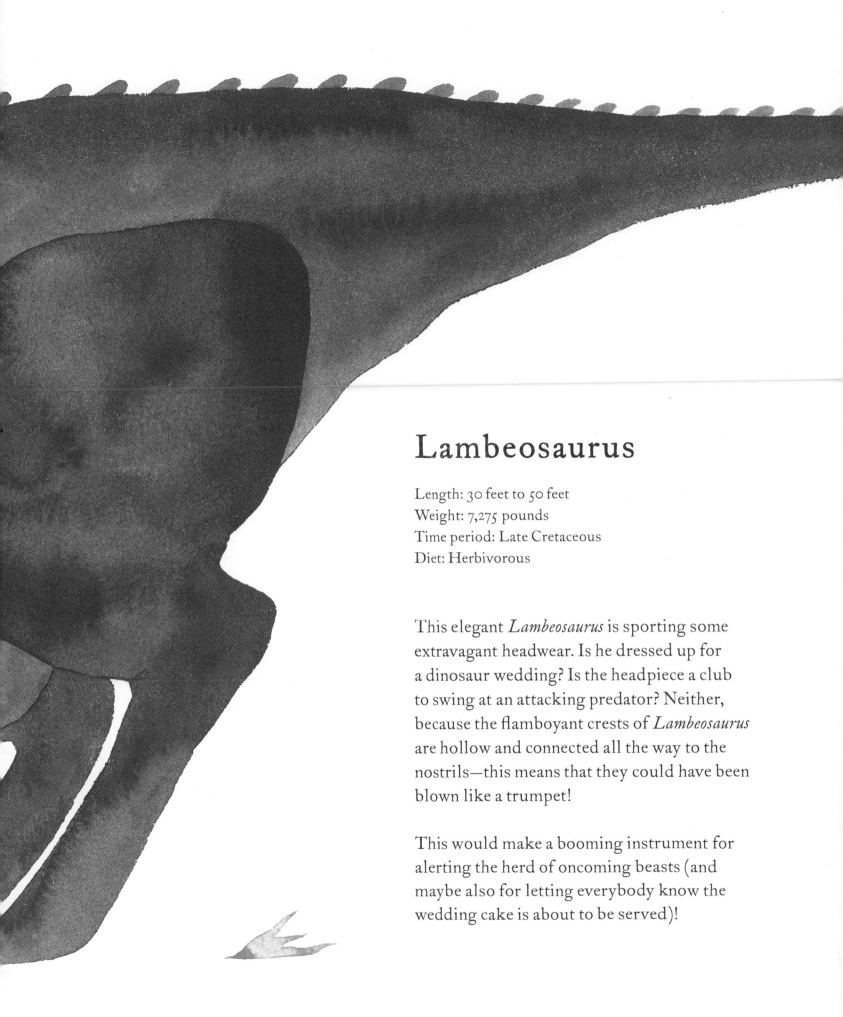

Lambeosaurus

Length: 30 feet to 50 feet
Weight: 7,275 pounds
Time period: Late Cretaceous
Diet: Herbivorous

This elegant *Lambeosaurus* is sporting some extravagant headwear. Is he dressed up for a dinosaur wedding? Is the headpiece a club to swing at an attacking predator? Neither, because the flamboyant crests of *Lambeosaurus* are hollow and connected all the way to the nostrils—this means that they could have been blown like a trumpet!

This would make a booming instrument for alerting the herd of oncoming beasts (and maybe also for letting everybody know the wedding cake is about to be served)!

Amargasaurus

Length: 40 feet
Weight: 12 tons
Time period: Early Cretaceous
Diet: Herbivorous

Amargasaurus is the oddball of the sauropods—millions of years younger and much shorter than its ancestors, it had an wicked set of neck spikes. Extra security for protection from predators? *Amargasaurus* also had a sail up his back, perhaps for display or regulating heat. It has been suggested that the sail continued up both sides of the neck—it must have been hard to concentrate on eating leaves when your head was being blown about on a windy day!

Triceratops

Length: 25 feet to 30 feet
Weight: 15½ tons
Time period: Late Cretaceous
Diet: Herbivorous

The saberlike horns and huge neck frill of *Triceratops* have made its face one of the most recognizable of the Cretaceous period. However, *Triceratops* is only one member of the similarly featured ceratopsid family, which also includes *Machairoceratops* and *Einiosaurus* (see pages 40–41).

For years the mighty neck ruff was believed to be a defense against the chomping *Tyrannosaurus*, but now it is thought that they had a more decorative function. Just like antlers, these magnificent displays were probably used to ward off predators, or were used by males to attract female *Triceratops*. Fossilized skulls have revealed many different types of ceratopsian headwear, such as the downward nose horn of the *Einiosaurus*. The odd curved spikes of the *Machairoceratops*, whose name means "bent swords," were discovered only in 2016. Who knows what else is waiting to be discovered?

Machairoceratops

Length: 20 feet to 25 feet
Weight: 4,400 pounds to 5,500 pounds
Time period: Late Cretaceous
Diet: Herbivorous

Einiosaurus

Length: 15 feet to 20 feet
Weight: Estimated 4,400 pounds
to 6,600 pounds
Time period: Late Cretaceous
Diet: Herbivorous

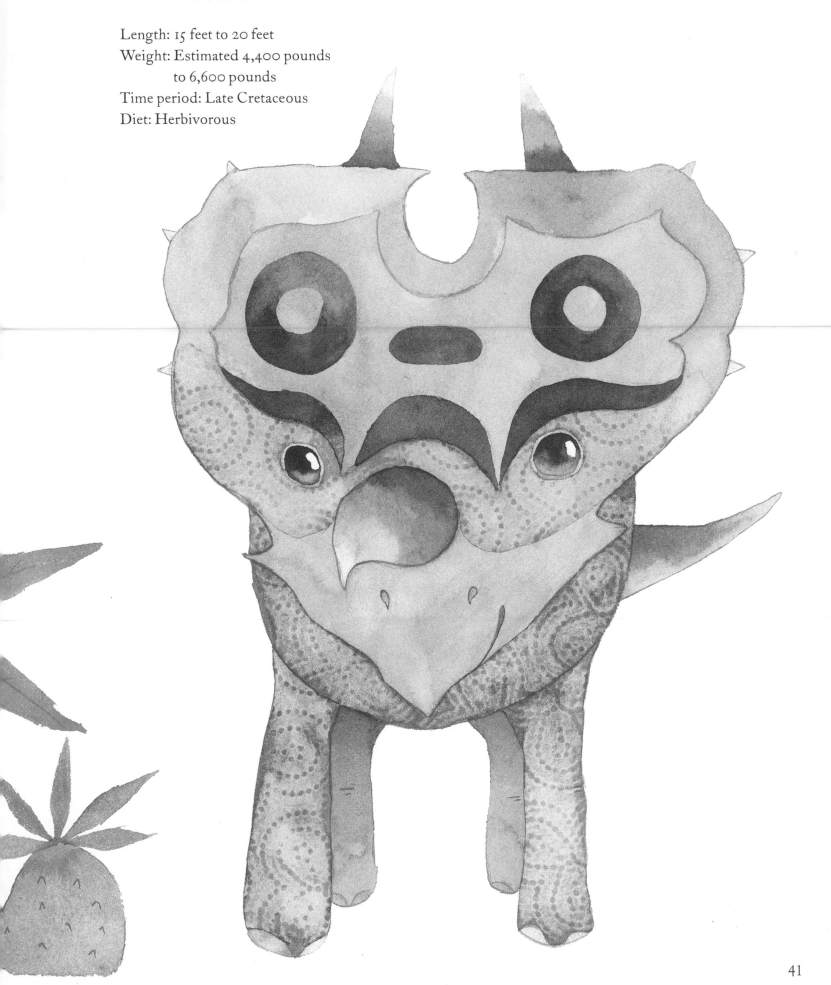

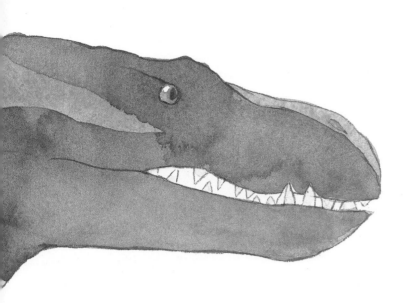

Tyrannosaurus rex

Length: 40 feet
Weight: 8 ¾ tons
Time period: Late Cretaceous
Diet: Carnivorous

The king of the predators, the queen of fear—
Tyrannosaurus is undeniably dinosaur royalty. Perhaps
the most famous dinosaur ever, the commonly
known *T. rex* was a killing machine from what is
now North America. The end of the long line of the
tyrannosauroidea ("tyrant lizards") family, this mighty
predator had evolved massive bone-crushing jaws, with
teeth the size of this book.

But then an asteroid came along and let the more
birdlike dinosaurs take over!

PS: A similarly fearsome dino called *Giganotosaurus*
roamed South America thirty million years before
T. rex's day. Also at about forty feet long, this huge
bipedal predator could have taken *T. rex* on for size!

Yutyrannus

Length: 30 feet
Weight: 3,000 pounds
Time period: Early Cretaceous
Diet: Carnivorous

Did the feared tyrannosaurs have feathers? A 2012 discovery of the Chinese "feathered tyrant" *Yutyrannus* has proved this strange theory correct! This thirty-foot monster's fossils show a complete feathered covering, and because the *Yutyrannus* has been dated earlier than its famous cousin, the two dinosaurs may have shared this evolutionary trait.

Or perhaps that part of China was colder than the *T. rex*'s American turf, so it needed a cozy feathered jacket to keep warm.

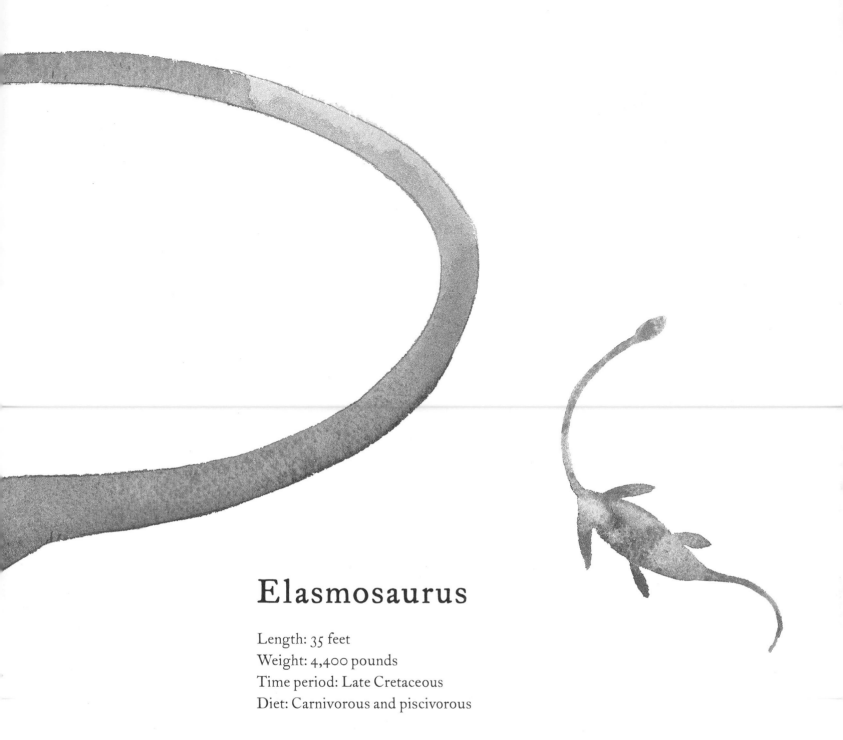

Elasmosaurus

Length: 35 feet
Weight: 4,400 pounds
Time period: Late Cretaceous
Diet: Carnivorous and piscivorous

The traditional silhouette of the *Elasmosaurus* is well known to dinosaur fans—which is funny, because they were not dinosaurs but plesiosaurs! This unique shape is characteristic of plesiosaurs, and the Late Cretaceous *Elasmosaurus* is a prime example.

It was a fast swimmer with powerful paddles and an extra-long neck for catching shoreside fish. It was more like a speedboat close to the beach than a whalelike battleship far out in the big blue sea.

Dromiceiomimus

Length: 11 feet, 6 inches
Weight: 285 pounds
Time period: Late Cretaceous
Diet: Omnivorous

Creatures such as *Dromiceiomimus* make it easy for us to see the links between birds and dinosaurs. This dinosaur was part of the ostrichlike ornithomimosaur family—all fast running and fine feathered.

Because they could top forty-five miles per hour, they could easily outpace predators, and they also used their large eyes and beaks to spot and catch fast lizards. Those poor lizards didn't stand a chance.

Tupuxuara and Tapejara

Wingspan: 16 feet, 5 inches
Weight: 45 pounds to 75 pounds
Time period: Early–Middle Cretaceous
Diet: Carnivorous and piscivorous

Wingspan: 11 feet, 8 inches
Weight: 90 pounds
Time period: Early–Middle Cretaceous
Diet: Carnivorous and piscivorous

The skies above the shores and beaches of the late Jurassic and early Cretaceous periods would have been as full of creatures in flight as our seashore is today. Unlike our modern-day birds, these two didn't have a feather between them, only skin stretched from their fingers and arms and amazing headwear made of bone. Both *Tupuxuara* and *Tapejara* may have had crests that could change color for courtship displays. They certainly look a lot more colorful than our boring white gulls, but with a wingspan of up to fifteen feet, they were a lot more threatening too.

Yingshanosaurus

Length: 13 feet to 16 feet, 5 inches
Weight: 2,200 pounds to 3,000 pounds
Time period: Late Jurassic
Diet: Herbivorous

This spiky stegosaur is an early
ancestor of the famous plate-backed
Stegosaurus. Stegosaurs lived all
over the world, but many species
have been found in China—such as
this *Yingshanosaurus* and its cousin
Tuojiangosaurus. *Yingshanosaurus*
had impressive shoulder spikes,
a striking but clumsy look that
didn't take off in Late Jurassic
fashion season!

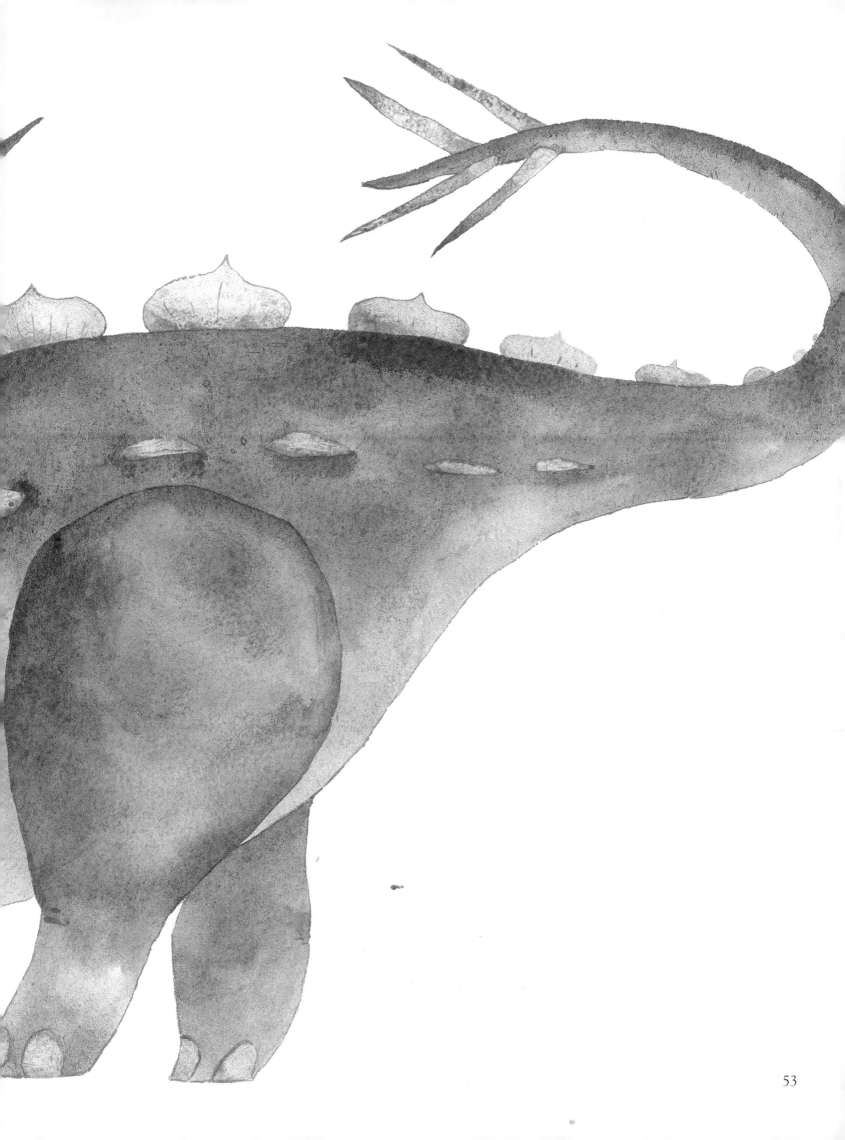

Brachiosaurus

Length: 85 feet
Weight: 61¾ tons
Time period: Late Jurassic
Diet: Herbivorous

The Jurassic *Brachiosaurus* was certainly
not the largest sauropod, but it did have
uniquely long front legs, meaning that its
back was steeply sloped.

Brachiosaurus had a number of look-alike
family members with some odd names,
such as *Supersaurus* and *Giraffatitan*—they
could only be huge dinosaurs with names
such as these!

Troodon

Length: 8 feet, 3 inches
Weight: 110 pounds
Time period: Late Cretaceous
Diet: Omnivorous

The troodontids of the Cretaceous period were a family of clawed, fast-running, feathered dinosaurs with forward-facing eyes—it's handy to have binocular vision for hunting. *Troodon* is particularly interesting due to its large brain, which is thought to be the largest brain-to-body weight ratio of all dinosaurs. But if we remember that *Troodon* had a brain the size of a chicken's, we can be reassured that these "birds" aren't exactly rocket scientists!

Archaeopteryx

Length: 1 foot
Weight: 10 ½ ounces to 1 pound
Time period: Late Jurassic
Diet: Carnivorous

In 1861, a 150 million-year-old fossilized feather was found in Germany, sparking years of scientific debate and even playing a major role in Charles Darwin's theory of evolution. *Archaeopteryx* was the size of a blue jay and—aside from its dinosaur teeth, tail, and claws—was so birdlike that it clearly plays an important role in explaining the evolution from dinosaurs to birds.

For a long time, *Archaeopteryx* was even considered to be the oldest-known bird, but recent finds in China may have given that award to *Anchiornis*, a dinosaur or bird (still being debated) that predated *Archaeopteryx* by ten million years.

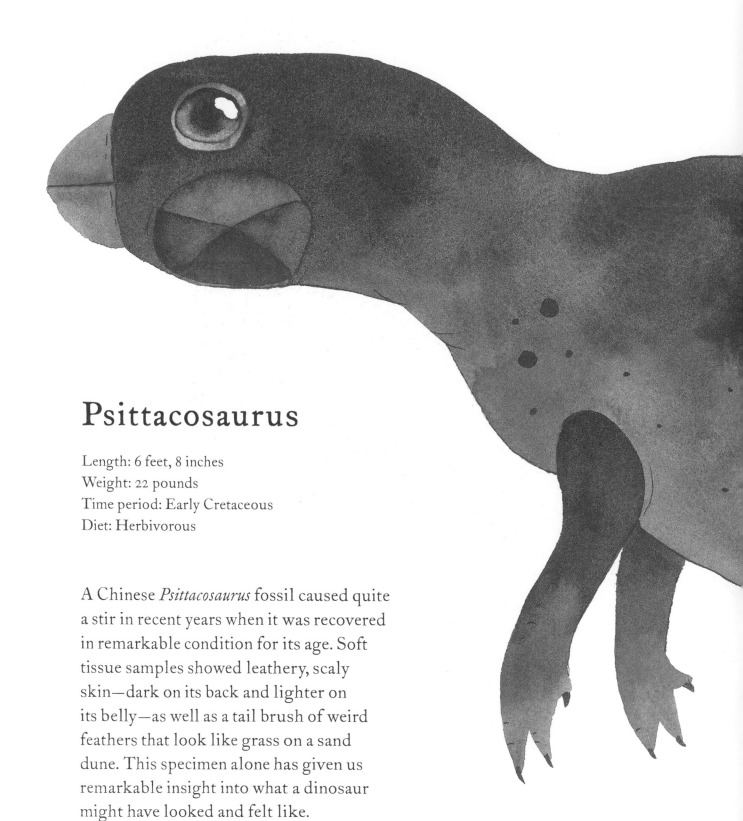

Psittacosaurus

Length: 6 feet, 8 inches
Weight: 22 pounds
Time period: Early Cretaceous
Diet: Herbivorous

A Chinese *Psittacosaurus* fossil caused quite
a stir in recent years when it was recovered
in remarkable condition for its age. Soft
tissue samples showed leathery, scaly
skin—dark on its back and lighter on
its belly—as well as a tail brush of weird
feathers that look like grass on a sand
dune. This specimen alone has given us
remarkable insight into what a dinosaur
might have looked and felt like.

Pachycephalosaurus

Length: 13 feet
Weight: 815 pounds
Time period: Late Cretaceous
Diet: Herbivorous

As well as the thick-skulled domes of their boneheaded family, the peaceful *Pachycephalosaurus* evolved crowns of thorns and piercing spikes. These ornaments of terror gave the teenage *Pachycephalosaurus* the name *Stygimoloch* ("the horned devil from the river of death"). When they grew into adults, they lost their horns.

Until recently, *Stygimoloch* and *Pachycephalosaurus* were considered different dinosaurs, but they probably represented different growth stages—together with the juvenile *Dracorex hogwartsia* ("the dragon king of Hogwarts")!

Fantastic names for a fantastic creature!

Tanystropheus

Length: 20 feet
Weight: 300 pounds
Time period: Middle Triassic
Diet: Carnivorous and piscivorous

Don't be fooled into thinking that this is a friendly baby diplodocus; the reptile is a dangerous adult fish-catcher. At twenty feet long and practically all neck, *Tanystropheus* would wait on the coastline of modern-day China and Italy to dart in and catch passing fish like a heron. Fish are slippery customers, so the extra-long neck would have been handy for the eventual underwater chase for dinner.

Baryonyx

Length: 30 feet
Weight: 6,400 pounds
Time period: Early–Middle Cretaceous
Diet: Carnivorous and piscivorous

In 1980s southern England, a set of bones unlike any other was discovered. The find included a narrow crocodile-like skull with bunched spiky teeth and an immense claw on its thumb, giving the beast a name meaning "heavy claw." Although not related to the crocodile, which lived at least seventy million years earlier, *Baryonyx* and crocodiles had a lot in common due to their ability to hunt and catch fish. Those English *Baryonyx* fossils were even unearthed with fish in the belly—but not with French fries!

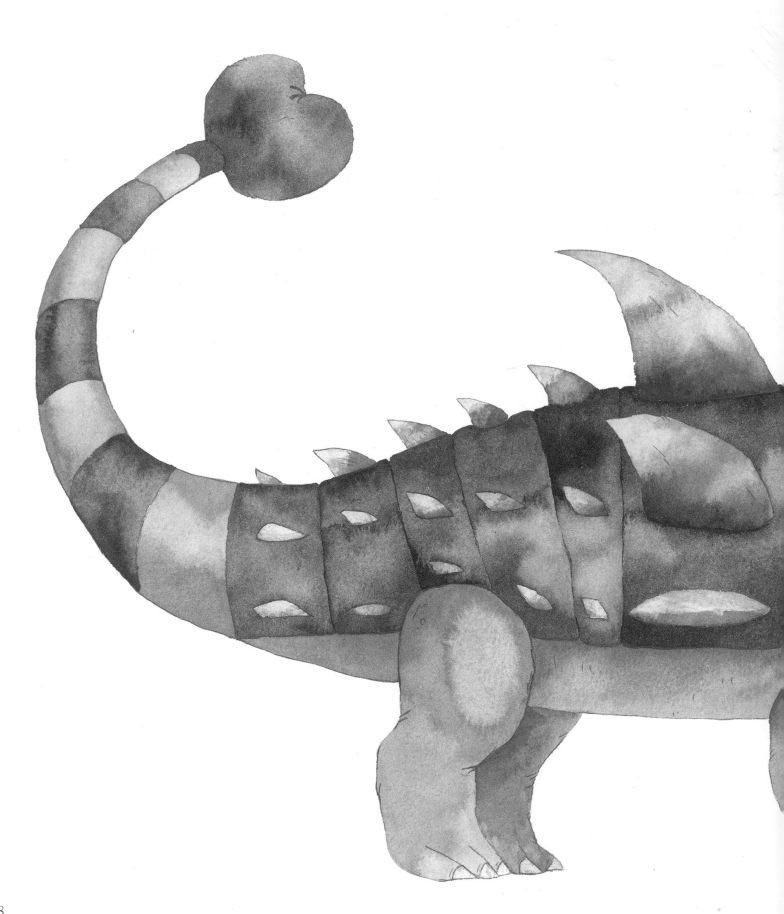

Euoplocephalus

Length: 16 feet, 5 inches to 23 feet
Weight: 5,000 pounds
Time period: Late Cretaceous
Diet: Herbivorous

Nobody has been able to say for sure what colors *Euoplocephalus* was, so these shades could just be an accurate representation!

You have to admit that, even without the sporty color palette, it is a cool dinosaur, armed to the teeth and ready for anything. Part of the ankylosaurid family, they were all covered in bony plates studded with huge spikes, and they had great swinging tails—not unlike a hefty brick at the end of a rope. This is definitely the guy to accompany you for protection when you're off to the stores and there's a rogue *Tyrannosaurus* about!

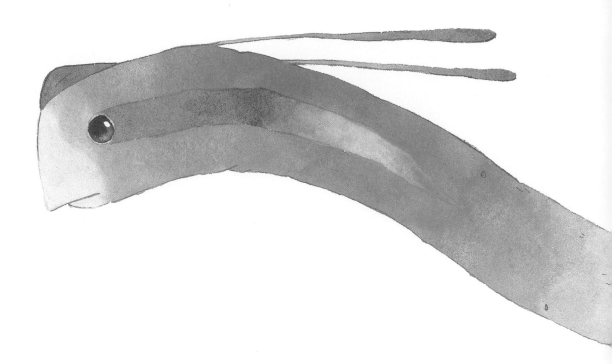

Khaan

Length: 6 feet
Weight: 60 pounds
Time period: Late Cretaceous
Diet: Omnivorous

Like *Nomingia*, this oddball was also a member of the curious oviraptorid family. Mostly found in China and Mongolia, oviraptorids all had long feathery tails, feathered arms and bodies, and toothless beaks. *Khaan*, whose name means "warlord," looks less like any other traditional dinosaur and more like a roadrunner that has collided with a wall.

Europasaurus and Magyarosaurus

Length: 20 feet
Weight: 2,200 pounds
Time period: Late Jurassic
Diet: Herbivorous

Length: 20 feet
Weight: 1,650 pounds
Time period: Late Cretaceous
Diet: Herbivorous

These two small sauropods, each no longer than twenty feet, would struggle to reach the leaves of many trees. They were fairly similar, except for the subtle armor of *Magyarosaurus* (showing its titanosaur roots) and a difference of fifty million years.

Aside from their diminutive size, they also had in common their small island homes. Food in these places was minimal, so these dinosaurs had to buck the trend for large sizes and keep themselves short and sweet.

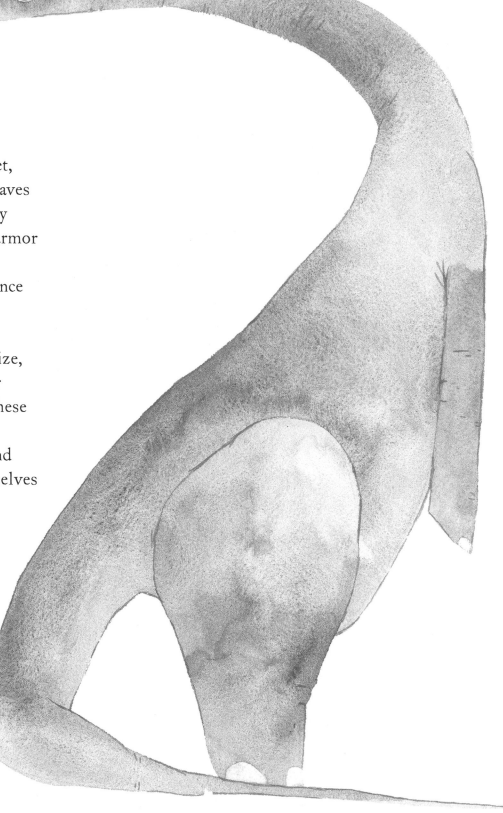

Dracoraptor

Length: 6 feet, 8 inches to 9 feet, 9 inches
Weight: 20 pounds to 45 pounds
Time period: Early Jurassic
Diet: Carnivorous

Dracoraptor may be this book's most recently discovered dinosaur; the first fossils were found in coastal Wales in 2014. Two fossil-hunting brothers revealed to the world a teenage dinosaur from the Jurassic period, more than two hundred million years old. The brothers paid tribute to the Welsh Dragon with a name from the Latin *draco* ("dragon").

It's great to know that, once upon a time, dragons really did roam the Welsh valleys!

Mosasaurus and Basilosaurus

Length: 55 feet
Weight: 5 ½ tons
Time period: Late Cretaceous
Diet: Carnivorous

Length: 60 feet
Weight: 7 ¾ tons
Time period: Late Eocene
Diet: Carnivorous

The oceans of the Late Cretaceous period were home to some of the largest and scariest creatures to ever stalk our waterways. Millions of years after the age of the ichthyosaur, these new dangers included *Mosasaurus*—a brutal predator with the appearance that was part crocodile, part shark. These fearsome beasts were about sixty feet long, meaning that they were three times the length of our present-day great white shark.

The much younger but similarly fearsome *Basilosaurus* may have been given a dinosaur name, but this early ancestor of the whale was a mammal, unlike the reptilian *Mosasaurus*.

The goliath *Basilosaurus* was a top hunter of its time—somewhat like a killer whale, but three times as big and with jaws that would have been able to snap anchors.

Pterodaustro

Wingspan: 8 feet, 3 inches
Weight: 11 pounds
Time period: Early Cretaceous
Diet: Carnivorous

As we have seen, the pterosaurs of
the Cretaceous period had developed
all kinds of weird add-ons and
appendages. *Pterodaustro* had a mouth
like a brush for straining water for
tiny seafood, just like the whales and
flamingos of today. It has even been
considered that *Pterodaustro* may have
been pink like a flamingo, due to its
similar diet.

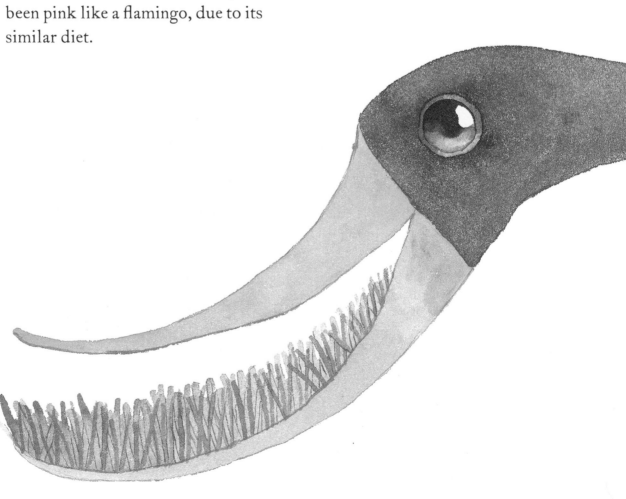

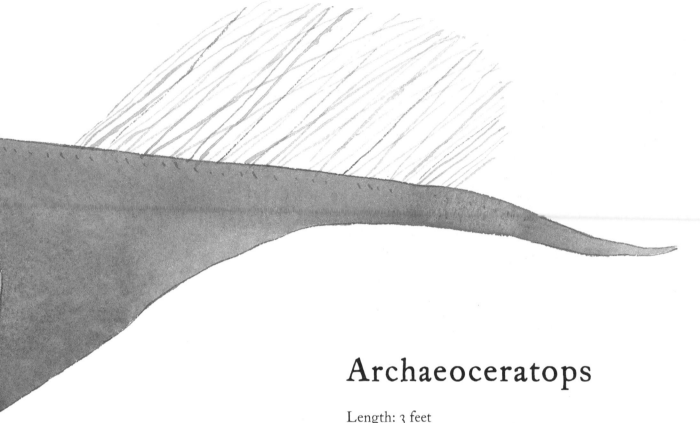

Archaeoceratops

Length: 3 feet
Weight: 20 pounds
Time period: Early Cretaceous
Diet: Herbivorous

This curious little dinosaur is part of the
evolutionary chain of the mighty *Triceratops*.
His name, meaning "ancient horn-face," sums
him up. His head does look ungainly with such
a skinny body! He would surely have to be
extra careful in the school playground to avoid
getting his head stuck between the rails. Quick!
Call the fire department!

Gigantoraptor

Length: 26 feet
Weight: 4,400 pounds
Time period: Late Cretaceous
Diet: Carnivorous

With a name like *Gigantoraptor*, it's not hard to guess that this beast was worryingly large. This big bird cast a huge shadow over the rest of the oviraptorid family because—at his weight and height—he was more than four times the size of them!

However, the creature did have most of the family traits—beak, feathers, tail, and name. The oviraptors, or "egg plunderers," were given this name because it was thought that their beaks were used for raiding and eating other dinosaurs' eggs.

This has since been proven wrong, and probably for the best, because it would have taken two dozen *Argentinosaurus* eggs to fill this *Gigantoraptor* at breakfast!

Therizinosaurus

Length: 40 feet
Weight: Estimated 2,200 pounds to 6,600 pounds
Time period: Late Cretaceous
Diet: Thought to be herbivorous

The first fossils found of this peaceful herbivore were of its imposing three-foot-long claws. Strangely, the scientists at the time thought they belonged to a turtlelike creature wading around on the seafloor. Weird.

Eventually, the scientists figured out this was a forty-foot-tall tree lover that liked nothing better than using those curved claws to cut down branches and reach the tasty tops that nobody else could stretch to.

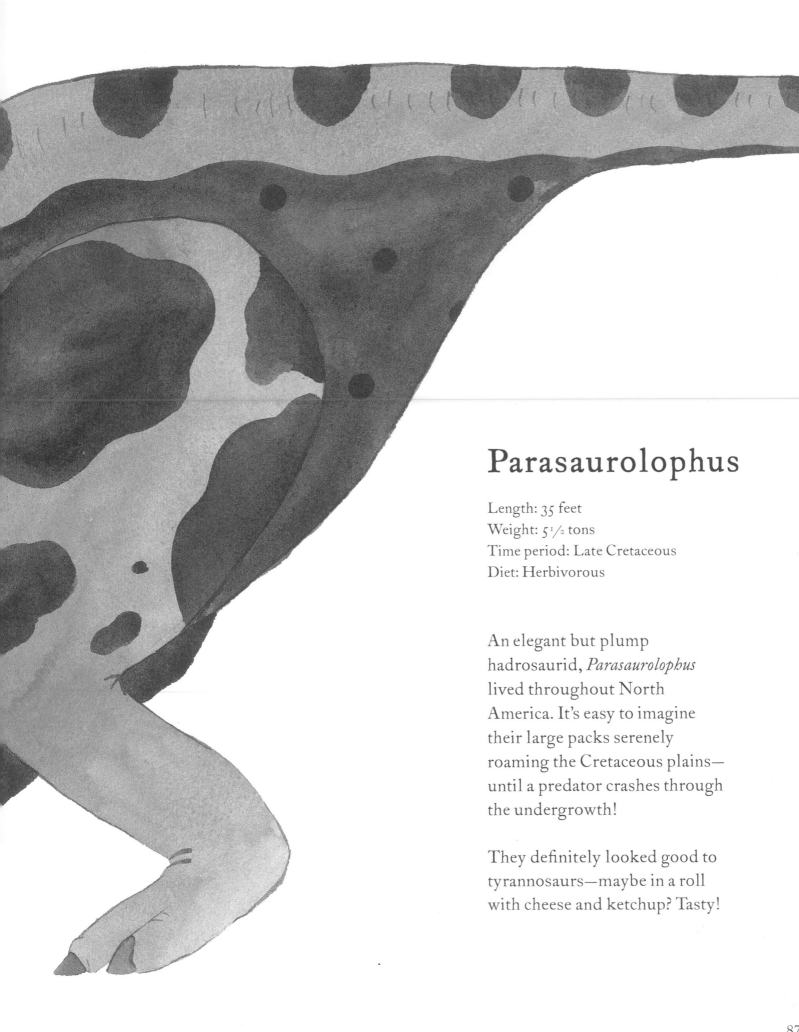

Parasaurolophus

Length: 35 feet
Weight: 5 1/2 tons
Time period: Late Cretaceous
Diet: Herbivorous

An elegant but plump
hadrosaurid, *Parasaurolophus*
lived throughout North
America. It's easy to imagine
their large packs serenely
roaming the Cretaceous plains—
until a predator crashes through
the undergrowth!

They definitely looked good to
tyrannosaurs—maybe in a roll
with cheese and ketchup? Tasty!

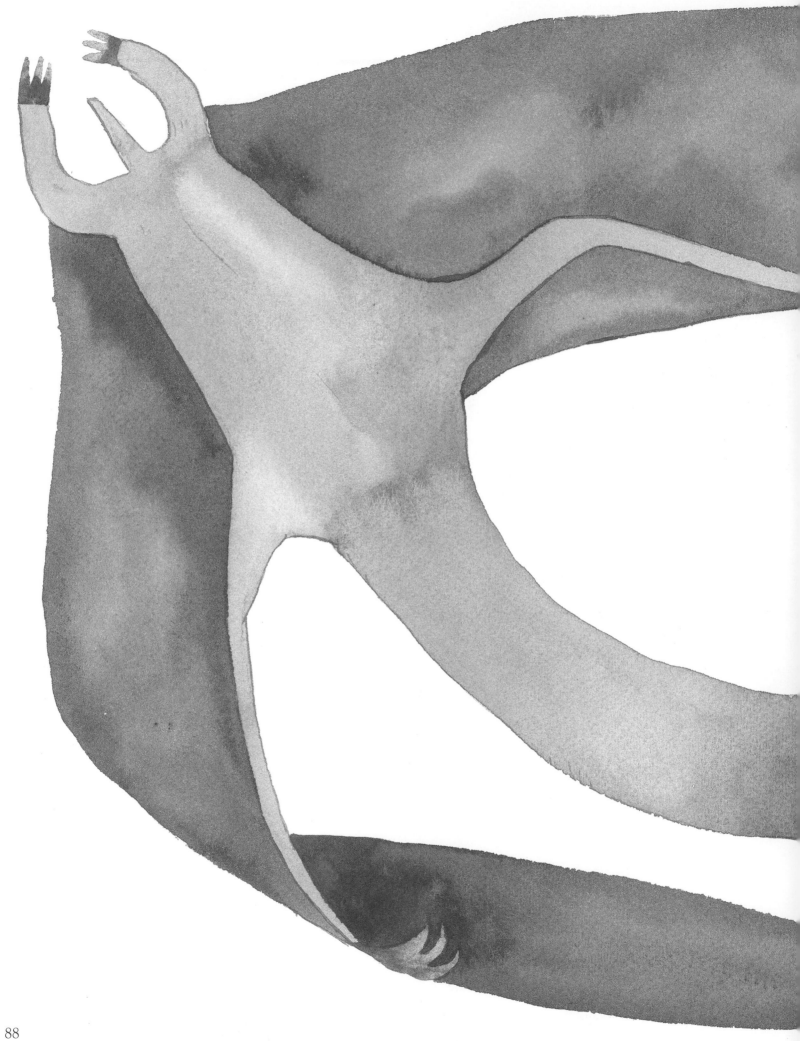

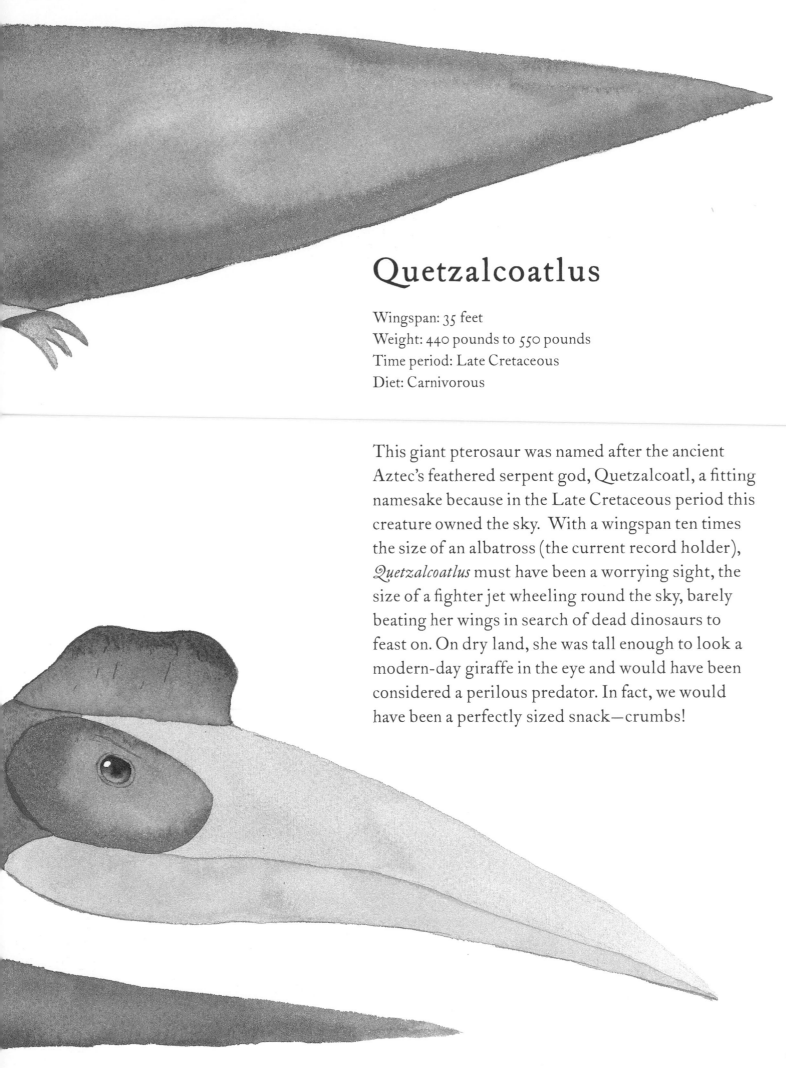

Quetzalcoatlus

Wingspan: 35 feet
Weight: 440 pounds to 550 pounds
Time period: Late Cretaceous
Diet: Carnivorous

This giant pterosaur was named after the ancient Aztec's feathered serpent god, Quetzalcoatl, a fitting namesake because in the Late Cretaceous period this creature owned the sky. With a wingspan ten times the size of an albatross (the current record holder), *Quetzalcoatlus* must have been a worrying sight, the size of a fighter jet wheeling round the sky, barely beating her wings in search of dead dinosaurs to feast on. On dry land, she was tall enough to look a modern-day giraffe in the eye and would have been considered a perilous predator. In fact, we would have been a perfectly sized snack—crumbs!

Microraptor

Wingspan: 2 feet, 5½ inches
Weight: 4 pounds, 6 ounces
Time period: Early Cretaceous
Diet: Carnivorous

Microraptor was unearthed in China a few years before *Gigantoraptor*, in the early 2000s. This dinosaur was around the size of a pigeon, and it displayed aerodynamic and wing-structured feathers on all limbs.

It is thought that they would have glided from tree to tree, much like flying squirrels. It's a good look that it is rarely seen anymore; time and nature have shown us that two wings are better than four.

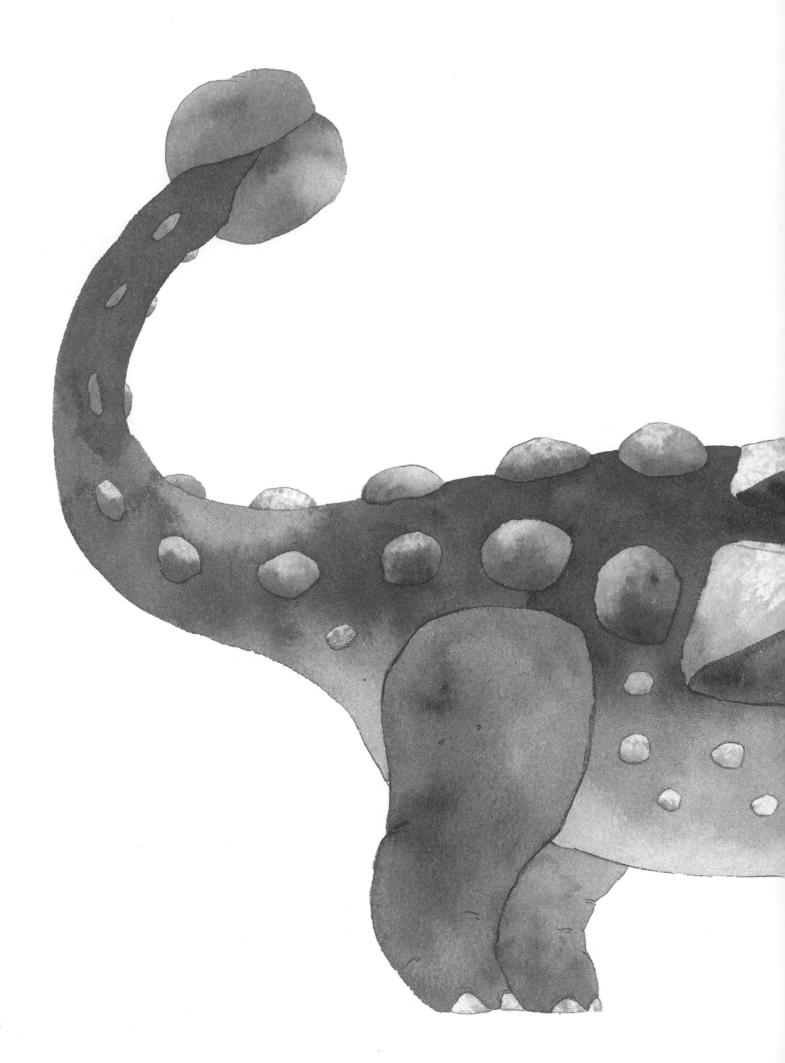

Ankylosaurus

Length: 20 feet to 23 feet
Weight: 5 ¼ tons
Time period: Late Cretaceous
Diet: Herbivorous

The big-boned, low-slung *Ankylosaurus* probably
never called on speed or agility to get out of a
difficult situation. It's handy they were covered
in fused bone, protecting them like the pads on a
football player's uniform. The shields look pretty
heavy, so it was a good thing that they could use their
tail club as a weapon—the size of a trash-can lid!
They probably couldn't knock out the thick-domed
Tyrannosaurus, but they could definitely snap a few
ankles before shuffling off somewhere safer.

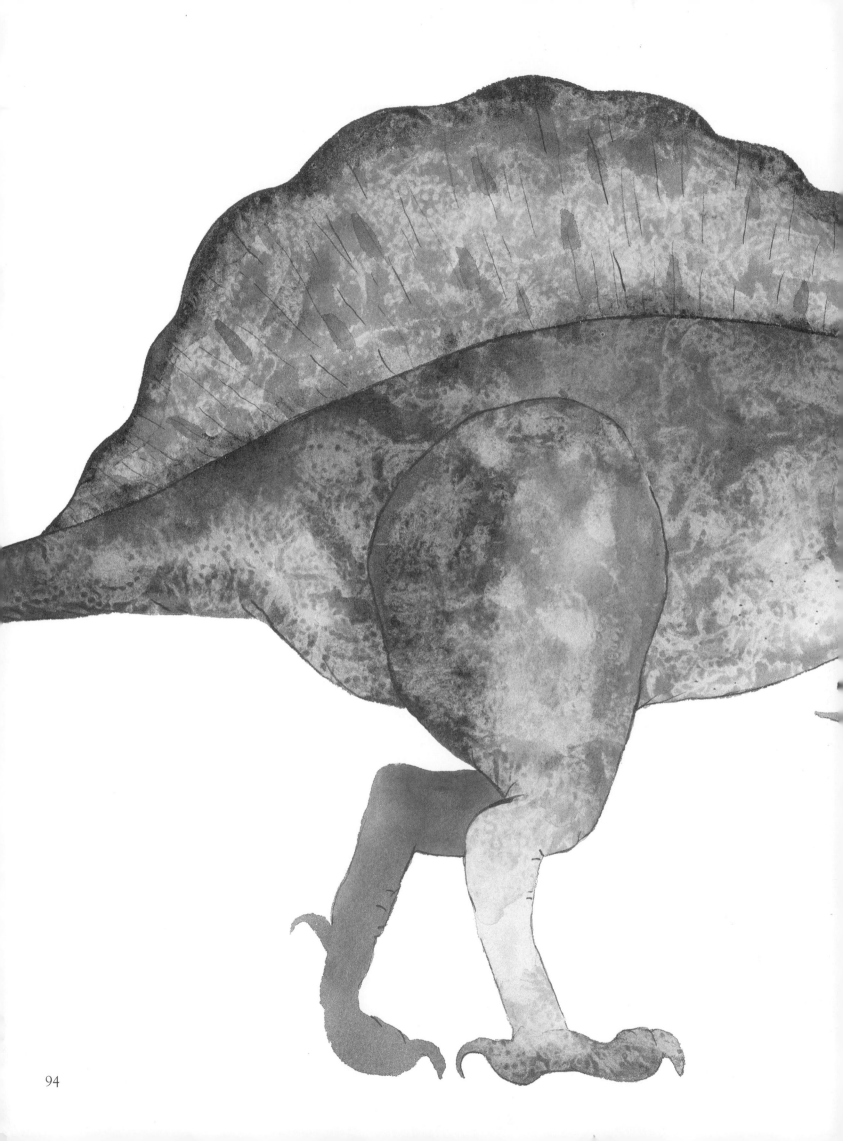

Spinosaurus

Length: 40 feet to 55 feet
Weight: 6 ⅔ tons
Time period: Early–Middle Cretaceous
Diet: Carnivorous and piscivorous

If you thought that a twenty-foot Australian saltwater crocodile was enough to make you quake in your boots, imagine your fright as a fifty-five-foot *Spinosaurus* stomps through the swamps toward you. ARGH! This monster had a flat head full of pen-size teeth, a hideous sail on its back, and was bigger than *Tyrannosaurus*. This guy would have been king of the swamps—I'm sure nobody would try and stand in its way.

Thank yous

To Jess, for her unending love and support, and Romy, Mae, and Bonny, for the good times.

To the Sewells, the Lees, the Roses, and the O'Sullivan-Averys.

To Dr. Stephen Brusatte, University of Edinburgh; Psittacosaurus model maker, Robert Nicholls; West Midlands Safari Park; and the Natural History Museum.

Published by
Princeton Architectural Press
A McEvoy Group company
202 Warren Street, Hudson, NY 12534
Visit our website at www.papress.com

First published in 2017 as *Dinosaurs and Other Prehistoric Creatures* in Great Britain by
Pavilion Children's Books
43 Great Ormond Street, London WC1N 3HZ
Princeton Architectural Press edition published in 2018

Design and layout © 2017 Pavilion Children's Books
Text and illustrations © 2017 Matt Sewell
All rights reserved
Printed in China
21 20 19 18 4 3 2 1 First edition

ISBN 978-1-61689-716-1

Princeton Architectural Press is a leading publisher in architecture, design, photography, landscape, and visual culture. We create fine books and stationery of unsurpassed quality and production values. With more than one thousand titles published, we find design everywhere and in the most unlikely places.

No part of this book may be used or reproduced in any manner without written permission from the publisher, except in the context of reviews.

Every reasonable attempt has been made to identify owners of copyright. Errors or omissions will be corrected in subsequent editions.

For Princeton Architectural Press:
Editor: Nina Pick

Special thanks to: Ryan Alcazar, Janet Behning, Nolan Boomer, Abby Bussel, Benjamin English, Jan Cigliano Hartman, Susan Hershberg, Kristen Hewitt, Lia Hunt, Valerie Kamen, Jennifer Lippert, Sara McKay, Eliana Miller, Wes Seeley, Rob Shaeffer, Sara Stemen, Marisa Tesoro, Paul Wagner, and Joseph Weston of Princeton Architectural Press
—Kevin C. Lippert, publisher

Library of Congress Cataloging-in-Publication Data available upon request.